ESSAY SERIES

Contract Killing in the Information Age
by Jason Ray Forbus

ISBN 9788833461175

Graphic design and layout: Sara Calmosi

Ali Ribelli Edizioni
Series – Essay
www.aliribelli.com – redazione@aliribelli.com

Contract Killing in the Information Age

by Jason Ray Forbus

MSc in Globalization
University of Aberdeen, United Kingdom

AliRibelli

FOREWORD

> A street thug and a paid killer are professionals - beasts of prey, if you will, who have dissociated themselves from the rest of humanity and can now see human beings in the same way that trout fishermen see trout.

So speaks the American psychiatrist Willard Gaylin. His view seems to confirm one of the many myths and legends that surround the mysterious figure variously known as the professional (or hired) killer, the assassin and the hit man. Such a person is widely thought of in modern society as standing alone, outside of the common run of humanity, coldly and calculatedly observing fellow human beings as if they were animals to be hunted or as mere objects to be manipulated at will.

Such a view is perpetuated in countless popular fictions. At the current time the comprehensive online film database IMDB lists 1015 movies that have the keyword 'hit man' attached to them. The related term 'assassin' yields some 841 films that concern such a figure. The majority of these films seem to date from the last twenty years or so, indicating that the hit man has become one of the central figures in contemporary popular culture, ranking along other sinister but compelling personages as the zombie and the vampire.

Something about modern popular culture finds the professional killer a highly fascinating figure, a character that is constantly resurrected and reworked, from the existential loners of *Le Samourai* and *Ghost Dog*, to the 'ordinary' guys who just happen to murder for a living, as in *Grosse Pointe Blank*. Perhaps the key characteristic of the fictionalised assassin is his (or in the case of *La Femme Nikita*, her) cool. This is coolness in two senses: the level-headedness needed to make a hit successfully, evading capture and pocketing the fee; and the coolness of the lone individual handling high-specification, hi-tech hardware with minimum fuss and maximum expertise and precision. Any fool can (mis)handle a gun, says popular culture; but only the hired killer knows and understand the aesthetics of the rifle barrel and the silencer, the silence of the kill, and the cleanliness of a job well done. If we were to believe what we watch and what we read in films and magazines, the professional killer is cool personified, walking and shooting cool.

This myth has particularly been proposed, reiterated and reworked since the 1960s. The two great source-texts are these. First, the films of Jean-Pierre Melville (such as *Le Samourai* noted above), where trench-coated, trilby-wearing assassins stalk the streets of Paris, presented as emblems of humankind's existential predicaments – the human creature quite alone in a world not of his own making, at odds with and utterly removed from all other human beings. Melville can be credited with turning the Sartrean existential individual of the 1950s into a hired assassin, a person whose one meaningful connection with other people is when he trains his sights upon them. The author major source of the modern fetishisation of the hired killer as the epitome of cool is Frederick Forsyth's *The Day of the Jackal*, turned into a highly influential film in the early 70s. As the Jackal speeds around summertime Italy and France in his open-top white convertible, preparing the means for an impossible hit – the assassination of de Gaulle – the viewer is left to wonder – could I do that? Could I kill people – rich and powerful people, perhaps wicked and depraved people – for a living? Even the most mild-mannered person may be tempted to engage in such thoughts, even just for a moment. Popular culture has set up the assassin as a powerful attraction figure, someone who – at least in the best cases – is truly Nietzschean, being thoroughly beyond good and evil. The assassin, like God, sits in judgement on the lives of those below him. While God sees all from the sky or some transcendent viewpoint, the professional killer sees all through his telescopic sight, while perched on a rooftop. Like God's the hit man's gaze is downward and panoptic, as well as being able to home in on the minutest details of its target. There are theological resonances in how we imagine the doings and characters of those who kill for money.

It is particularly remarkable that the hitman should have such a positive image. Of course, one need not be a fully paid-up Lacanian to realise that popular culture is full of the most peculiar perversities. After all, the serial killer is widely presented as someone that has a certain sort of allure, from the warped morality of a Dexter to the ineffable charm of Hannibal Lecter. But the striking thing is how the generally positive myths of the assassin developed at a time when 'real life' assassins were set up as demon figures. The 1960s was the decade of the great modern assassinations, at least in the US. That country had a track record in such a direction, of course, pioneered by the likes of John Wilkes Booth ruining President Lincoln's enjoyment of the show. But the assassins of JFK, Martin Luther King and Bobby Kennedy seemed, when caught or dead, to be the kind of pale, squirming, inadequate creatures one would find under a stone. When they were not projected as evil personified, they were represented as being far too lacking in substance properly to be called anything like evil. It was their pathetic nature that was the striking thing, said journalism of the time. While the movie assassin was becoming the essence of style, the likes of Jack Ruby and Lee Harvey Oswald were its opposite. It is in retrospect very noticeable how the fictional assassin remained untainted by his real-life counterpart's glaring inadequacies. Of course, the real assassins the public knew about were the failed ones – the ones who had been caught. They could hardly be set up as successful practitioners of the art of death. But the paradox is that it was in a period when the real assassin is seen to be a grubby lowlife that the fictional killer should start to take on the qualities of a kind of Superman.

It is into this odd but fascinating terrain that Jason Forbus boldly steps. His work is an attempt to go beyond the stereotypes of popular fiction about the hired killer, finding the more complex realities that are at play within their (under)world. This is a bold project, not least because academia and assassins make unlikely, indeed uneasy, bedfellows. (This was particularly acutely dramatised in 2010 when a Pennsylvania sociology professor was suspended by her university's authorities because she had jokingly written on a private Facebook entry that she wanted to hire a killer who could erase some of the people who had made her day less than great – clearly the assassin is appealing as long as s/he keeps to the confines of the television screen, but any hint of her entering campus life is a cause for great alarm.)

The one major sociological treatment of hired killers I am aware of is Ken Levi's 1981 paper 'Becoming a Hit Man', which traces out how apprentice assassins reconfigure their worldviews so that their consciousness – and consciences – become systematically re-attuned to the demands of their new occupation. Levi's paper is empirically fascinating but remains hemmed in by the standard concepts and concerns of American symbolic interactionist sociology of the time. Forbus, by contrast, has ranged much wider, both in space and in time.

As regards the latter, he exhibits a strong historical and comparative sensibility. We can indeed, as he avers, only really understand the social institutions and practices of hired killing in our own era if we look at previous historical periods and their characteristic forms of socially ordering paid-for death – examining such characteristic groups as the ronin of medieval Japan through to the Mafia hit squads of the mid-20th century America.

In terms of ranging spatially, Forbus has particularly wanted to understand how globalization processes are today implicated in hired killing. This seems to me a particularly interesting and provocative contribution to the now vast literature on globalization. As the work of scholars like Federico Varese (2011) indicates, it is not just that criminal organisations are affected by globalization; they also play an important role in shaping processes of globalization. How can we understand the nature of Russia today except by understanding how, through the world-shattering events involved in the fall of Communism, new forms of intimidation, extortion and killing for money were created? Likewise, no understanding of contemporary Latin American modernity can fail to mention the particular modes of assassination and death produced by the strong globalization of the drugs trade. Indeed, once one begins to think about – and it is precisely these issues that Forbus challenges us to contemplate – the entire world social system today is thoroughly bound up with and depends on different types of murder-for-pay, from mass killings in Mexico to the poisoning of Russian dissidents and the mysterious deaths of investigative journalists.

Two provocations follow, it seems to me, from such considerations. First, is the hit man not the cousin (or the twin brother) of the soldier, who also takes money to kill his or her fellow human beings? The soldier's murdering is wrapped in a flag, just as the hit man's doings may be enmeshed in a code of honour and pride in doing a clean job – both are forms of self-justification in the act of slaughter. Second, is this a golden age of the assassin, a period of particularly unpleasant social conditions, where gangster capitalism is the norm and feral elites have shed any semblance of previous attempts to veil their naked greed, lust for power and shameless disdain of the mass of the population? Capitalism and hired killing have long gone hand in hand. It should therefore not be so surprising that the globalised turbo-capitalism of today should be apparently providing so many job opportunities for old hands and new guns in the assassination business.

As you read Forbus's work, you may find yourself thinking along these lines or on many others. Whatever you take from it, one thing is clear - his writing has significantly helped us to realise that the hired gun is not just a person who entertains us on the page or on the cinema screen, but rather is simultaneously a real person, a set of activities, and a complex assembly of social relations, all intimately bound up with wider social, political and economic dynamics. Whether we are thrilled by the prospect or appalled at the thought, the professional killer is among us today, in all sorts of ways, some more apparent and many more opaque. This work helps shine the light of analysis into that troubling but compelling opacity.

References

Levi, K. (1981) 'Becoming a Hit Man. Neutralization in a Very Deviant Career', Urban Life, 10 (1): 47-63

Varese, K. (2011) *Mafias on the Move: How Organized Crime Conquers New Territories*, Princeton: Princeton University Press

David Inglis
Professor of Sociology
University of Aberdeen

ABSTRACT

This dissertation discusses the ancient profession of the hit man from its early, mythical origins to our present day. By drawing from a literature comprising of historical sources, US Secret Service data, and auto-biographies of renowned hit men, the paper will first provide an approximate understanding of these law-offenders by looking at their backgrounds and goals, and then compare their characteristics to those expressed by "make-shift killers." Hence the paper will aim at defining that 1) our modern, business-oriented society is affecting the modus operandi adopted by freelance professional killers in reaching their clientele, which often resembles the customary approach of other legally recognized professions, and that 2) due to astounding improvements in transport and communication technologies, hit men are becoming further delocalized from their areas of origin to operate on a truly global scale. Data at hand, the dissertation will finally argue that with modern wealth and opportunity, hit men are no longer restrained to work for criminal organizations, politicians or businessmen, but have become available to an ever-growing and varying demand, thus following the democratizing process undergone by other professions.

Key words: democratization, globalization, hit man, postmodernity.

Contents

I

Introduction

They have been called many names throughout history: assassin, ninja, killer, gunman, hit man, and as they are sometimes referred as in our business-obsessed society, "hired to kill" or, rather ambiguously, "independent contractors." Yet, their role has stayed true to its original intent, that is to murder for financial gain or other benefits. By no means an all-inclusive work, the aim of this dissertation is to prove that what has changed are the modus operandi adopted by professional killers and their clientele.

Perhaps the earliest-recorded[1] instance is the murder of Moabite King Eglon by Ehud around 1337 B.C. Although its truthfulness is highly debatable, it is nonetheless the first written account – and a truculent one, at that – we have of an assassination. This was no minor accomplishment, neither. As the story goes, Ehud was sent by God Himself to assassinate Eglon and thus deliver the Israelites from the Moabite yoke. In this case the assassination clearly served a higher purpose, and was destined to result in great political consequences. What this account also tells us, regardless of its historical reliability, is the role held by assassinations in Ehud's society in terms of the relevance of the

[1] The Book of Judges

feat and of the parties involved. In fact, it goes without saying that in the ancient world the great majority of people were so poor and underprivileged that assassins sole source of work were royals (or gods).

As society evolved, and masses acquired more financial independence, eventually their motivations and desires for personal vendettas did too. It is perhaps a direct consequence of the complexity of our current age that, along with the nature of the clients, their motivations to hire a hit man have also greatly diversified. No longer is the work of a hit man bound to political assassinations – although these still enjoy the privilege of the headlines – but it bounces from one trivial matter to another. From the more worrisome activities of criminal organizations to the broken-hearted man who seeks revenge on his ex-wife, our "independent contractor" has become a freelancer with a busy agenda, fixed tariffs, and modus operandi. He, the Hit Man, is the paradoxical epitome of modern opportunity.

Weaknesses and method

The main difficulty encountered while collecting the data was, surprisingly enough, the data itself. Literature based on professional killers is extremely scarce and often comes in the form of appendixes to broader studies dedicated to private mercenary companies, criminal organizations, serial killers, and famous assassinations of public figures. Getting hold of information about independent contractors – that is freelancers who will "hit" anyone for a price and know no loyalty beside hard cash – was therefore arduous, and in this aspect the confessions of famous hit men such as Tony "the Greek" Frankos, together with investigation leaks published on a number of newspaper articles, have proven essential in the development of this dissertation.

The paper is divided into the following sections: a brief "historical background of contract murder", where the origins of hired murder are analyzed, and a particular emphasis is given to the localization as opposed to delocalization of hit men, their weaponry, and clients; "life of a hit man", instead, looks at the particular stories of each individual, and their possible responsibility in turning a man into a hirable murderer and an outcast; "the required traits of a hit man" focuses on the characteristics that are normally sought in a hit man; "postmodernity" defines the contemporary stratagems adopted by independent contractors, and the extent of their relation to organized crime; lastly, drawing from the previous sections, the "conclusion" will establish the main topic of the dissertation.

II

Historical background of contract murder

With the extraordinary invention of agriculture over 10,000 years ago, the destiny of the human race was about to change forever. The initial transformation from a nomadic to permanent settler existence resulted in the inevitable complication of societal needs. A tribal chief was no longer able to respond to the growing demands of a swelling, varied population, and a political structure soon developed under the aegis of religion.

Things like arts, culture, law, religion and science, that is all that defines us as humans, soon came into existence. The harvesting of crops and the storage of agricultural surpluses, on the other hand, created the first form of accumulation known and consequently wealth (North and Thomas, 1977). This rudimentary wealth gave origin to the market as people exchanged goods for other supplies, and around 5,000 B.C. the first coins appeared, moving the market from the practice of bartering to the purchase of goods in exchange for money. However, wealth and power, accompanied by an inadequate judicial system inevitably triggered social injustice. To survive in a ruthless society, the poorest sections of the citizenry often became indebted and were obliged to renounce to their very basic rights to become slaves at the service of wealthy masters. In other cases, a foreign invasion could turn an entire population into slavery.

Such was the tragic case of the Israelite people around the 12th century B.C., when the Moabites conquered the land of Israel and began a period of oppression. Under the Moabite domination, the Israelites were forced into paying tributes and serve their foreign masters as slaves. Not all hope was lost though, as a man named Ehud prepared himself to deliver the Israelites from the Moabite yoke. According to the Book of Judges, God personally chose Ehud because of his left-handedness, thanks to which he was able to conceal a double-edged dagger on his right thigh (Book of Judges, 3:16) and sneak past King Eglon's guards. Once he was in the presence of the King, Ehud thrust the weapon in his belly (Book of Judges, 3:21), thus murdering the royal and effectively bringing the Moabite domination to an end. Little could the murderer know that his feat was destined to become the first of a long, infamous list of famous killings, and albeit its historical truthfulness is highly debatable, the name of Ehud passed on to history as the first recorded assassin.

At this time in history, assassination served the whims of politics and religion, which often were one and the same. However, assassination was not limited to the land of Israel, and throughout history it has been utilized by men with no scruples and liberators alike to gain power or subvert the constituted order. A short list of assassinations and failed attempts is therefore presented to prove this assertion.

In 227 B.C., as far East as China, a scholar and a swordsman named Jing Ke from the state of Wei, refusing to become a slave at the service of the Qin state and with the benevolence of his king, attempted to assassinate the Emperor. The mission, however, failed and the perpetrator was executed (Qian, 109-91 B.C.). Had Jing Ke's attempt succeeded, the entire history of China might have followed a different course.

The year 44 B.C. arguably records the most famous assassination in history: the murder of Gaius Julius Caesar, Dictator of Rome, at the hands of several Senators among whom the main conspirators were Marcus Junius Brutus and Gaius Cassius

Longinus (Suetonius, 109 B.C.). The assassination of Caesar eventually resulted in the end of the Roman Republic.

One of the first ever recorded assassinations carried out by an individual specifically trained to kill, however, dates back to 1092 a.D, when the powerful Seljuk vizier Nizam al-Mulk was murdered by an Assassin in Baghdad. The vizier became the first victim of this radical sect of Islam known as Ismailism that, through a fatal combination of murder and diplomacy, managed to play a prominent role in the turbulent political structure of Persia and the Middle-East for the next two hundred years (Lewis, 2002). So infamous were the gruesome feats of this sect, that their appellative Asasyun, literally meaning "people who are faithful to the Asās" (foundation of faith), came to denote, in its English equivalent word "one who murders by surprise attack, especially one who carries out a plot to kill a prominent person" (The Free Dictionary, 2011). Furthermore, learning how far and wide Assassins were willing to travel in the pursuit of their missions was at the very least surprising. Once the Imam – the chief of the religious community known as Umma – assigned him a target, the Assassin would hop on a horse and leave for his destination. Thus, avoiding the cities and stopping along the way at fortresses controlled by allied Ismaili communities, the Assassin would travel as far as Syria, Palestine, and Afghanistan to carry out a hit (Lewis, 2002). Once he reached his destination, the Assassin would normally benefit from a secret Ismaili network firmly established in the area, thanks to which he would learn everything there was to know about the target. The meticulousness with which Assassins carried out their missions included behavioral studies and linguistics, of which the famous assassination of the King of Jerusalem Conrad de Montferrat in 1192 represents a prominent case: disguised as Christian monks, two Assassins attacked King Conrad, stabbing him to death before his own elite guards. Put under torture, the Assassins claimed that the hit had been ordered by King Richard the Lionheart. The King of England, however, declined any responsibility in the matter. The involvement of Richard in the assassination of Conrad is still debated by scholars; if the confession of the Assassins was to be true, not only the entire history of the Christian Occupation of the Holy Land would have to be rewritten, but – more relevant to the argument of this dissertation – the Sect of the Asasyun would assume a different connotation, and resemble a group of freelance professional killers rather than a religious sect. However, British-American historian Bernard Lewis (2002), regarded as one of the West's leading scholars of the Middle-East, rejects any involvement of King Richard as inaccurate and forged by the political rivalries of the time.

Around the 14th century, another group of individuals highly specialized in espionage, sabotage, infiltration, and last but not least assassination, emerged in the turmoil of feudal Japan (Turnbull, 2007). These mysterious warriors were referred to with a variety of names, among which shinobi (meaning "one who steals away") was the most widely used. However, in the aftermath of World War II, the word ninja – "one skilled in the art of stealth" – became more prevalent than shinobi, probably because it was easier to pronounce for Western speakers (Turnbull, 2003: 6). Ninjas rather than assassins are the rightful predecessors of modern hit men, and the reason why will now be explained.

Although similar in their approach to warfare through their usage of disguise, secrecy and surprise attack, there are a number of striking differences setting Assassins apart from Ninjas. First and foremost, Assassins were not mercenaries for hire: they fought and willingly martyred themselves in the hope to bring into power Ismailism, the second largest branch of Shia Islam, a belief system that focuses on the deeper, esoteric meaning (batin) of the Islamic religion (Lewis, 2002). Assassins did not murder for personal gain, but fought for what they considered a higher purpose. Death on mission was motive of pride for the family of the Assassin, who were supposed to accept the orders of their lords regardless of the risks involved. In this sense,

Assassins are much closer to our present day terrorists than to professional killers. Lastly, Assassins only utilized daggers that had been specifically "consecrated to the mission" to fulfill their murderous duty.

Ninjas, on the other hand, were not believers intent on bringing into being a new religious order, but mercenaries providing their sought after services to the highest bidder. Their loyalty lied with their clan alone, whose elders trained them to become cunning spies and silent killers. In this aspect, ninjas predated the sense of loyalty shown by present day Yakuza gangsters toward their criminal organization. The arsenal of ninjas consisted in a wide array of weapons, ranging from daggers and katanas – the latter being their symbolic weapon – to darts, spikes, knives, poison, caltrops, landmines, firearms and many others (Mol, 2003: 124). Far from being limited to a "consecrated dagger", then, ninjas had no reservation in utilizing whatever mean allowed them to fulfill the mission in the most secretive and effective of ways.

Even so, assassins and ninjas did share some common traits. Ninjas operated indifferently throughout feudal Japan. Some warrior lords stationed their ninjas in faraway cities, relaying information by lighting signal fires on mountain tops (Adams, 1966: 19) and other secretive means. Like assassins, then, ninjas could rely on a thick network of fellow spies and be ready to strike at any time their contractor commanded. Another similarity between assassins and ninjas lies in the fact that they were usually born and raised within such a community. Similarly to Assassin fortresses, Ninja villages were localized in specific areas, identifiable with the modern Mie Prefecture and the bordering region of Kōga.

The cases mentioned this far have focused on the political and religious motivations for assassinations. Crime, however, has always been the major source of income for hit men. Historical sources in this regard are, however, scarce. Horace (65-8 B.C.) described two professional killers, named Apollodorus and Canidia, who carried out numerous "contracts" with deadly hemlock imbued with honey (Newton, 2008: 23). Albeit certifiable empirical data in regards to hits in the ancient world are practically non¬-existent, assuming that criminal entrepreneurships have long utilized professional killers to extend and maintain their underworld supremacy is by no means a blasphemous statement.

Unfortunately, in the past 150 years, the Sicilian Mafia and other criminal organizations from Southern Italy overfill this informational gap. Like Japan, feudalism in Southern Italy had a long-lasted existence, arguably enduring to this day in the form of labor exploitation to which tens of thousands of illegal immigrants are forced into. Cosa Nostra – "Our Thing", as Sicilian Mafiosi address their own organization – emerged during the turmoil caused by the transition from feudalism in 1812 and the conquest of the island by mainland Italy in 1860. The newborn government redistributed the land of nobles to private owners, whose total number increased from 2,000 to a staggering 20,000. With nobility gone from the lands, however, so did their private armies. At this time of deep social unrest and unemployment, many young peasants joined into groups of bandits and roamed the country (Bandiera, 2001). In the meanwhile, the police force was unmanned and unable to respond to the problem. The absence of a state whose far north capital based in the industrial city of Turin well represented the detachment of the political establishment from the concerns of its most backwards regions, and the stark North-South divide reigning in the country since its early beginnings, together with the desperate need for protection against an endemic banditry, is what ultimately urged the Sicilian elites to ask for protection to "companies-at-arms", often constituted by ex-convicts who were suddenly getting paid for what they did best: kill. Predictably, it did not take long for these "companies-at-arms" to turn from solution into a problem (Lupo, 2009). Once common banditry was wiped out from the island, the reason to be for these companies ceased to exist. But, rather than disband and seek an honest trade, in the majority of cases its affiliates resorted to a new strategy: protection, they would assure to land-owners and store-keepers, was still necessary. Ironically, these companies offered protection from the violence perpetrated by their own affiliates and rival companies; failing to pay for this protection would result in sabotage and murder. Mafia, enriched by the protection racketeering it had set up, soon developed into a number of clans and branched out to other criminal trades. The plight of Southern Italy had begun and a new category of specialized killers emerged: the mafiusi – a Sicilian adjective that derives from the slang Arabic marfud, meaning "swaggering" or "boldness, bravado" – ruthless criminals who swear allegiance to a padrino (godfather) and carry out whatever order it is given to them, regardless of the cruelties they are asked to commit (Servadio, 1978). Mafiusi call themselves "Men of Honor", and normally follow the rule of umirtà ("code of silence") that prevents them from becoming pentiti (turncoats). Breaking umirtà results in the death of the turncoat and his family; this "code of silence" is also imposed on the general population under the same penalty. It is thanks to this regime of fear that Cosa Nostra has been able to maintain its grasp over Sicily during the last one hundred and fifty years.

Dictator Benito Mussolini had no sympathy for Cosa Nostra, which he considered – justly so – an overt threat to his authoritarian rule. In January 1925, Mussolini appointed Cesare Mori as the Prefect of Palermo. The order appointing Mr. Mori to the task left little doubt about what was required of him:

> 'Your Excellency has carte blanche, the authority of the State must absolutely, I repeat absolutely, be reestablished in Sicily. If the laws still in force hinder you, this will be no problem, as we will draw up new laws.' (Mussolini cited in Petacco, 2004: 190)

To our present day the most effective and brutal war against Cosa Nostra, the campaign led by the "Iron Prefect" Mori almost succeeded in annihilating the criminal organization by torturing, imprisoning and executing hundreds of Mafiosi. Those who did manage to escape the law either went undercover or fled to the United States of America, where Prohibition and the government's misled beliefs and underestimation of Mafia promised enormous and easy profits. Among the Mafiosi who reached the shores of the New World were Carlo Gambino and Joseph Bonanno, who would eventually become powerful godfathers in New York City. With the Diaspora of Mafiosi to the US, Canada and Australia, Cosa Nostra exported a criminal franchising and went global. The "global shift" of crime is closely related to and explains how contemporary hit men operate, and will be discussed in further detail in the chapters entitled "The required traits of a hit man" and "Postmodernity."

Nowhere was this criminal franchising more successful than New York City. As the presence of organized crime in the Big Apple increased, so did competition over the control of illegal and profitable businesses. However, bosses knew better than battling rival gangs with their own soldiers, strategy that would have resulted in the certain deaths of some loyal affiliates and an obvious connection to their own organizations, and eventually themselves. Therefore, the demand for highly qualified killers who were unaffiliated to any specific gang brought a team of ruthless criminals together and resulted in the foundation of the infamous group Murder Incorporated. Albeit they defined themselves as independent contractors till the very last, it is no mystery that the members of Murder Inc. worked closely with a number of Irish, Italian and Jewish gangs. Their organization, which was operative from the 1920s through the 1940s, ultimately worked for the National Crime Syndicate. Hits were discussed during the commissions of the syndicate, and subsequently reported to Murder Inc., whose members could be ordered to carry out a hit as far South as Florida, or as far West as Minnesota. Murder Inc. was so efficient in tracking down its targets, that it often outdone the police in the pursuit of law offenders. On top of that, the organization made use of a wide number of weapons, ranging from firearms to bombs. Fellow Murder Inc. hit man Harry "Pittsburgh Phil" Strauss, however, preferred the ice pick over any other weapon and paved the way to future, sinisterly creative assassinations.

Murder Inc. proclaimed itself as an "independent' group, but its main source of income remained tightly connected to criminal organizations from all over the United States. In a way, the group came to be recognized as the "long arm of the mob" (Crime Library, n.d.). What distanced Murder Inc. affiliates from "regular" Mafia hit men is the very same thing that defines them as the rightful predecessors of contemporary "independent contractors". Murder Inc. affiliates, in fact, had a system of tariffs (from $1,000 to $5,000 for a hit) and enjoyed fixed monthly salaries; after a hit had been assigned, the target's habits and whereabouts would be carefully studied until the killer resolved he ran no risk of getting caught. Only then the hit would be carried out, job done, contract terminated.

As the saying goes, "bad weeds never die". In the 1990s Perry Roark – also known as "Supermax Roark" – a white man being held at the Maryland Adjustment Correctional Center, expressed his wish to join the Black Guerrilla Family (BGF) but was denied entrance because of his skin color. For this reason, Roark founded Dead Man Incorporated (DMI), a white offshoot of BGF. The gang had two co-founders, James Sweeney and Brian Jordan, who the authorities sent to facilities in Texas and Louisiana, respectively in the vain hope of disrupting the gangs activities. However, data suggests that transferring the two co-founders only served to spread DMI's influence, which now counts on roughly 10,000 members nationwide (The Baltimore Sun, 2009). The main activities of the gang include contract murders on behalf of the BGF. The Black Guerrilla Family reportedly offered $10,000 to DMI to do hits on correctional officers and anyone else who helped with or conducted the investigation that resulted in the indictment of 24 alleged BGF members (Baltimore City

Paper, 2009). Founded and currently operating within prison walls, Dead Man Incorporated deals with murder in a somehow less efficient way than Murder Inc. However, as their infamous predecessors, DMI members also benefit from an underworld network through which they are able to obtain the information and the means required to carry out a hit.

Assassins, Ninjas, Mafiosi, DMI members: respectively soldiers at the service of a religious sect, a guild, and criminal organizations; they are different faces of the same coin. Modern hit men owe much to their infamous predecessors, and yet differ greatly from them for a number of reasons among which the lack of a targetable allegiance certainly constitutes the most obvious feature.

But where do hit men exactly originate from?

III

Life of a hit man

Writer and crime expert Gordon Kerr seems to have a clear understanding of what a client is looking for in a professional killer:

> [...] 'you would be looking for someone without a vestige of conscience or emotion. He or she kills coolly and calculatedly without stopping to think. It's just a job, after all. The moment a contract killer stops to consider the implications of a hit, or thinks too hard about a victim, his career is effectively over.' (2008: 8)

A lack of morality is therefore a necessary requirement to mercilessly murder a total stranger. Exactly how a man loses all morality, and decides to make killing his profession, is a matter that will be discussed in this section. As in the case of the men who joined the French Foreign Legion at the turn of the 19th and 20th centuries, what ultimately triggers individuals to reach such a life changing, extreme decision is a chain of events that looked at singularly do not tell us much, but when put together clearly pave the way to a criminal career as a professional killer. In this sense, the life of Donald "Tony the Greek" Georges Frankos, famous independent contractor, is illuminating.

Frankos was born in 1938 in Hackensack, New Jersey, to a Greek father and an Italian mother. Pain was the trademark of his life since its early beginnings, as his mother died shortly after giving him birth. Some years later his father – after facing various economic difficulties due to the Great Depression – suffered from a severe illness and also died. Donald and his sister Georgia were legally adopted by their uncle Gus, brother to their father, who painted bridges to make a living. Gus was an alcoholic, and a beast of a man at that. He would beat his wife regularly, and Donald and Georgia often followed the same fate for no other reason than to appease the man's violent outbursts. The house where they lived was a reign of terror, and with nowhere else to run to the children had to be quick in learning how to survive… or die. Georgia, however, suffered a much worse fate, as when she became a teenager her uncle began to sexually harass her. The sexual violence became more and more insistent, to a point where the man would feel no shame in molesting the girl in front of her brother Donald and his own wife. Donald's continuous attempts to free his sister, on the other hand, did not serve to much, as he was still underage and the laws of the time did not punish child abuse as efficiently as our current legislation does. When Gus escaped to Greece with Georgia, Donald decided to join the Navy and leave it all behind himself. But the US Navy of the time offered no solace to a man like him: thrown into the pit with felons who were serving time on the ship as sailors, and sent to far away ports where illegal trades such as gambling, prostitution, drug trafficking, and the basest of human activities were carried out in the open, Frankos slowly abandoned the last vestiges of societal restraint he still held. Moreover, the discipline imposed by Navy officers, cold and soldierly in the making, probably reminded Donald of the orders imposed on him by his uncle. All these factors put together pushed Mr. Frankos to commit his first known crime, a theft:

> 'To this day I don't know why I opted for much patently self-destructive, dead-end behavior, but for whatever reason, it presented the inauspicious beginning of my criminal career. Maybe I stole

> the $1,000 because I was fed up with the discipline of first home and then navy, or maybe simply because here was the largest amount of cash I'd ever seen.' (Headley and Hoffman, 1992: 28)

Pettier felonies would therefore pave the way to much more serious crimes, as Mr. Frankos acknowledges:

> 'Every cop knows this truth: a killer doesn't suddenly sprout full-blown. He commits other crimes first.' (ibid.: 35)

It is not hard to understand how a rational individual raised in a background of violence and suffering, put before the alternative of an honest, hard-earned misery on one hand, and an illicit trade that promises easy and immediate rewards on the other, will muse over the possibility of a criminal career. Some do so consciously, others unconsciously; the outcome, however, is the same: the desperate individual is likely to climb the criminal ladder one step at the time, and the distance he or she will cover is determined solely by his or her personal skills and luck. This holds true for any legal and illegal profession, where working as an independent contractor or as a hit man employed by the mob makes very little difference. Therefore, before earning himself a reputation for being a "tough guy", the hit man must pass a number of tests, involving the simple delivery of illegal merchandise such as drugs (in small quantities), pimping, collecting money for loan-sharks, and body guarding higher ranking gangsters. Sometimes, murder comes before body guarding, as throughout the years mobsters have become wary of those they can trust their own lives with. In this case, committing a murder earns the individual the full criminal citizenship; it is a sort of sinister curriculum vitae, a guaranty of qualification and trust that opens the doors that count for the hit man. Reputation in crime is everything, and it seldom takes the form of written recommendation letters – albeit some letters written in a coded language have been found in the hideouts of mobsters, such as the Sicilian "Boss of all Bosses" Bernardo Provenzano. The underworld utilizes a simpler, yet efficient system to organize its employment market: the ancient method of word-of-mouth.

> 'I made this underworld list of free-lance hitters. Word-of-mouth reports about no-nonsense actions in the slam and on the street got me on it, and the position was solidified and greatly enhanced by my overt, bone-deep hatred of rats [cooperators with the police, writer's note]. My having permanently silenced a few blabbermouths made a Mafioso in the market to farm out a hit feel safe picking me as his triggerman. The bosses knew they could count on my silence. They also felt that if they told me something I would never repeat it to anyone.' (ibid.: 130)

This system presents a disadvantage, however, as anyone from within the underworld, and for whatever personal gain, may spread false rumors about a rival hit man and bring about his downfall. "Blabbermouths", as Mr. Frankos refers to them, perhaps constitute the greatest menace threatening a professional killer, for their slander or confessions may cause his incarceration by the authorities or elimination by his own esteemed colleagues.

At this point, it is the slang utilized by Mr. Frankos that provides us with an interesting insight on his nature. In their numerous interviews with the subject, the authors noted a peculiar behavior: depending on the nature of the topic that was being discussed, Mr. Frankos would shift from the English of a well-educated individual to a street jargon:

> 'Frankos usually speaks in the language of an intelligent, well-read individual, which he is. But on occasion, when describing a crime or a particularly horrible prison experience, he reverts to the rawest language of the street. When this happens he transforms in an eye blink from cheerful next-door neighbor into a man who has killed, killed often, and enjoys remembering out loud.' (ibid.: XXVIII)

For the subject's own admission, the US Federal Prison System is meant to break any trace of dignity that the convict still has. There is no redemption to be found within the prison walls, and sometimes the jailhouse becomes yet another battlefield for the gang wars occurring outside in the streets. Until the 1990s – and perhaps to this day – there is ample proof that hit men remained operative even during their incarceration, as corrupt officials were bribed into letting them out for short periods of time, during which professional killers were able to commit a murder while retaining an adamantine alibi. Sometimes, hit men do not need bribing any official, as their designated victim is a fellow convict imprisoned in the same facility. This, as it has been discussed in the section "Historical background of contract murder", is what is currently happening in the United States, where the Dead Man Incorporated gang dictates a murderous law.

By looking at the last quotation, it may also be argued that the hit man is perfectly able to switch from an everyday language to a hoodlum's slang. The power over dialectic is a fundamental bolt in the self-defense mechanism Mr. Frankos has assembled together over the years. Perhaps it serves to protect him from the external world, helping him to be recognized as a wolf belonging to the pack, or perhaps it protects him from his own self. A shift in language would therefore represent a shift in personality: the evil deeds and the bad memories stay confined within the conscience of this Donald Frankos. It is a way as any other to keep sanity in a profession that threatens to drive any normal individual to the brink of madness. But what other devices does a hit man adopt in this regard?

> 'Ever since I'd started running with mob people, more than a dozen years earlier, I'd recognized that freelancing held the secret to maintaining sanity.' (ibid., 1992: 8)

Freelancing would therefore help the hit man to retain some control over his own life. Blind submission and obedience to a gang risks to ensnare the hit man into a web of loyalties that would ultimately result in losing any authority over his own actions. But every time he pulls the trigger, the mental walls the hit man has built around his conscience begin to shake. It is renowned that most hit men have a form of addiction, the most common of which is a dependence to alcohol, or other unsavory habits. As their activity and consequently their psychological stress increases, some hit men recur to stronger drugs like heroin.

> 'I went to sleep and woke up the next day feeling like Superman. My self-esteem peaked – what a treacherous narcotic this is! – and I believed I would accomplish anything. I knew other people became hooked on heroin but, just like them, I told myself I wouldn't.' (ibid.: 31)

However, even a drug as powerful as heroin may fail in providing the hit man with the stupor he needs to forget his crimes, and the very source of psychological distress he is subjected to may turn into its own solution:

> 'Not even heroin supplied a rush as powerful as the moments before a kill, adrenaline pumping, senses transmitting messages of astounding clarity, and fear. I had reached the top of my profession as a contract killer, living a luxury-filled existence, receiving respect from the crime families; and bone-deep I was afraid of losing it all, a guaranteed denouement if only once I hesitated, lost my nerve, or just plain fucked up. Every time I went on a job I had to psyche myself up, whip my mind and guts into an internal frenzy. Always, acute fear provided the motivating, driving force.' (ibid.: 10)

Once the hit man reaches this point, once he begins to actually enjoy killing, there is no turning back. He has become that cold, calculating killing-machine envisioned by Kerr as the perfect assassin. Lives as such no longer matter, and victims are reduced to roaming sheep, ready to be caught and slaughtered by a willing executioner. Deprived of fear, rage, or any other human passion for what matters, independent contractors are driven only by one thing: the rush of adrenaline before a hit. The best professional killers are the ones who crave for it, constantly, as drug-addicts seeking their dose. It is renown that many gang bosses, once they have reached the top of the criminal pyramid, still enjoy partaking in hits. Women, money, power: nothing for these consumed killers holds the same pleasure as murdering a fellow human being.

Yet another strategy utilized by hit men to remain sane is to construct a code of conduct for a profession that otherwise presents none. It is perhaps the most desperate measure adopted by an independent contractor in the attempt, often vain, of stabilizing his life, even giving it meaning.

> 'By establishing some guidelines – never murder anyone who didn't deserve it, and never, never hurt women or children – I kept the conscience my mother had stirred from revolting against the crimes I committed. And I really did stick to my self-imposed rules. Several times I didn't kill a woman, even though the danger existed that she would testify against me.' (ibid.: 67)

Mr. Frankos did not always follow the guidelines he had set for himself. On a couple occasions, and under a "regular contract", he partook in the killings of some would-be-witnesses against fellow gangsters.

But what are the differences – and similarities – between professional killers and those I previously referred to as "makeshift killers"? An intensive study carried out by Fein and Vossekuil (1999) explores the thinking and behavior of 83 persons known to have attacked, or approached to attack, a public figure. The authors studied each subject's motives, selection of targets, planning, communication of threat and intent, symptoms of mental illness and significant life experiences. In other words, this article was an extremely valuable source of comparison between different species of killers.

What becomes clear by reading this paper, is that – similarly to independent contractors –makeshift killers usually come from histories of depression. Some of them lost their jobs or families to a fatality, while others were mistreated or abused during their childhoods. Whether the loss was due to a tragedy or to their own ill behavior, and whether the experience of mistreatment has a factual basis in real life or lacks one entirely, these individuals feel as if they have been wronged and come to resent society for all of their misfortunes and failures, which they often attribute to a specific group of people (politicians, immigrants, women, etc.), upon which they fully invest their craving for revenge. It is so that:

> 'JD had lost a marriage (and his family), his job, and hope. JD had long been interested in movies about assassination and in weapons. He was driving aimlessly through the Southwest, feeling hopeless, when he began to think that by assassinating the President he would achieve three ends: (1) the country would no longer be taken in the wrong direction; (2) he would no longer be "nonentity"; and (3) he would be killed, ending his pain and misery.' (ibid.: 327)

Whereas other subjects, apparently successful in life, may experience the same sense of hopelessness felt by people who had a factual reason, albeit thoroughly misconceived, to despair and hate. Such is the case of FD (the researchers have kept the names of some respondents anonymous):

> 'FD, although married, steadily employed, and a member of a church singing group, perceived herself as unlovable and as a failure. FD, a history buff, felt unloved by her husband, and meanly treated and unappreciated by her demanding boss. She

> was in some pain from a chronic medical condition. FD began to read about the Civil War and John Wilkes Booth. She developed an interest in the lives of American assassins and read avidly about them. FD came to believe that she was like previous assassins, a "loser." FD determined to get herself "removed" from society by attacking a prominent public official.' (ibid.: 327)

A common pattern uniting these amateurish killers to professional hit men such as Tony "the Greek" Frankos, is their peculiar interest in the history of assassination and assassins. At some point in their lives, whether before committing a murder (as it is the case for amateurish killers) or afterwards (as for professionals), hit men become interested in the theory of assassination (how this interest actually develops, and the role attributed to it by criminologists and generally courts, will be discussed further in the following section). In any case, while unprofessional killers seek to gain notoriety, recognition, public attention and elevation of their personal status (ibid.) through a highly publicized murder, professional killers try their best to avoid the very same things.

The most careful planners are the subjects whose primary motive is money. Such is the case of an aspiring independent contractor, Charles Harrelson, hired to hit Federal Judge Wood Jr. Prior to carrying out the hit, Harrelson studied the routines of Judge Wood for months before committing the murder (ibid.). Another difference setting makeshift killers and independent contractors apart from each other, is that the first often wish to be killed in their attack or near-lethal approach, whereas hit men plan an assassination in every detail, and such a preparation always includes an escape plan.

At the same time, to spell out more forcefully the difference between independent contractors and killers affiliated to criminal organizations, it must be reasserted how the first develop and maintain a close relationship with the underworld, which serves them as a source for supplies and information, whereas the latter are fully immersed into it. The lack of a fixed loyalty to a gang provides independent contractors with a higher degree of decision-making in terms of which contracts to pick, price listings and strategies in comparison to gang-affiliated hit men, who are bound to the rules set by their superiors. The downside of independent contractors' unaffiliation to any criminal group, however, is a greater vulnerability to police investigations and eventually conviction. According to an exceptionally interesting research conducted by the Australian Institute of Criminology, the hits perpetrated by gang hit men generally target rival drug traffickers or members of an established criminal network, and the purpose of the killings is to silence said rivals or remove them from interfering with business (Mouzos and Venditto, 2003). Of the 15 cases analyzed by Mouzos and Venditto, in fact, 12 were still unsolved at the time of the data collection, which according to the authors is due to the fact that

> 'the instigator knows where to find a proficient 'hit man' or has sufficient links to criminal activity to avoid 'searching for a lead' or 'putting out the word'. (ibid.: 44).

Even more important,

> 'the fact that there were no reported or detected attempted offences in this category is not generally surprising from a law enforcement perspective. Persons operating within this category are not likely to assist police investigations and would be reluctant to come forward in the first place. This reluctance could stem from a number of reasons, which includes self-interest or preservation, as quite often persons with intimate knowledge of contracts in this category are heavily involved themselves in crime and criminality. Secondly, this category invokes a real fear amongst protagonists where disloyalty would almost certainly prove fatal'. (ibid.: 44)

As it was mentioned on page 12 of this paper, then, the 'code of silence' is an inescapable element of organized crime, a reassurance of complete trust from which gangsters at all levels benefit while being investigated. Independent contractors, on the other hand, maintain a superficial relationship with the underworld and their claim of not having any fixed loyalty can prove beneficial or damaging, depending on the perspective.

This section has argued that (1) independent contractors are often – if not always – distressed individuals who, during a specific time of their life, experienced hardships and despair; (2) similarly to private mercenaries, independent contractors tend to have received a military training that results fundamental in their ability to use firearms; (3) before committing their first murder, they normally commit pettier crimes; (4) the stressful nature of their profession pushes them to make an abusive consumption of alcohol or drugs, and develop a serious form of addiction; (5) lastly, some independent contractors attain themselves to guidelines they have set for their own selves, in the hope to gain some degree of control over their lives.

IV

The required traits of a hit man

Let us consider for a moment – for a fleeting moment, and just for the sake of understanding – independent contractors as workers involved in an honest trade. Local newspapers usually leave a few pages open to all sorts of ads, ranging from the publicity of a "Thai-Swedish massage therapist" to "Jack the Plumber" exceptionally low prices. Well, what if a professional killer, hoping to reach potential new clients, wanted to see his own ad published? What would he write then?

The characteristics sought by clients in a professional killer are many and varied. Considering the choices made by Mafia bosses in the recruitment of their assassins and a number of other factors, the independent contractor would – with all probability – write something along these lines:

Independent Contractor for Hire

Highly experienced professional offers his services at competitive prices. Absolute privacy and reliability guaranteed. Willing to travel. Deadlines maintained. Neat and clean job or your money back. Call 000-000-000 . First 5 customers will receive a 15% discount.

This fake ad is nothing else than a dark humored joke. However, the internet abounds with this kind of "jokes". In fact, there are several websites, such as "www.hitman.us", that draw on a widespread public fascination for professional killers. This morbid interest has been nurtured by films like "Hitman" (Gens, 2007) and a great number of fictional and allegedly non-fictional works, among which the infamous "Hit Man: A Technical Manual for Independent Contractors" (Feral, 1983). The book, that some unknown sources claim was written by a Florida housewife under the use of a pseudonym, caused a public hullabaloo when it was found to be used as a guide in a triple murder case in March 1993. Lawrence T. Horn confessed to have used the book as his guide in the recruitment of the killer, the ex-convict James Perry, and the planning of the murder of his ex-wife Mildred, his son Trevor, and nurse Janice Saunders. Horn was hoping to receive the proceeds of a trust fund that resulted from his ex-wife's suing a hospital over injuries to their son (The Washington Post, 1996).

This is not the place to discuss the controversial suit Rice V. Paladin Enterprises. However, the above mentioned case certainly raises interest over the contents of the book. What kind of tips does the manual provide to aspirant murderers? To begin with, the book asserts that

> [...] 'the professional hit man fills a need in society and is, at times, the only alternative for "personal" justice. Moreover, if my advice and the proven methods in this book are followed, certainly no one will ever know.' (Feral, 1983: p.4)

With this statement, the author affirms two points: first, that the independent contractor fills a societal need, and in this sense it reasserts the normalization of this criminal profession; and second, that the instructions contained within the book are such that a "faultless murder" may be easily planned and executed so that the authorities will never discover the identity of the perpetrator. The Horn case, together with the Robert Vaughn Jones case in 1999, are the known cases in which the perpetrators have admitted of having utilized the manual as a valuable source of information. However, the question arises on how many other unsolved murders and supposed suicides involved a careful study of this manual.

The book presents many characteristics attributed to real hit men. In the prologue, the fictional hit man reaches his intended destination on a plane, which reminds us that independent contractors often operate in regions far from their usual localities. An example of the global scale on which contemporary professional killers operate is given in "Professional Killers" (Kerr, 2008: 11):

> 'As Greenberg fell to the ground, blood oozing from several bullet holes, Tick-Tock was already on his way back to the East Coast, 2,500 miles away.'

Allie "Tick-Tock" Tannenbaum, a member of the infamous Murder Inc., was ordered to hit a potential witness named Harry Greenberg in 1939. Albeit Tannenbaum normally operated in Upper State New York, hitting Greenberg in his house in Los Angeles did not constitute an impediment, but rather an advantage: the professional killers of the time were coming to the realization that, thanks to the exceptional improvements that had been made in the transportation and communication technologies, great distances could be easily covered and at the same time granted the hit man a potential alibi. How was Mr. Tannenbaum supposed to be in Los Angeles if he was seen playing pool with his pals in a bar in Queens?

But in our present time, everyone can travel from one corner of the world to another, provided he possesses the financial means and the documentation necessary. What truly distinguishes an independent contractor from a regular passenger seated on a plane is therefore the art of disguise. As in the case of Assassins and Ninjas, professional killers must constantly keep their real identity secret and play by the role they have momentarily assumed. A skilful actor, the professional killer may have to interpret the role of a German businessman, or of a British holidaymaker to fulfill his contract. But pretending is not enough. Officials and customs require papers testifying about one's fake identity. For this reason, a forged passport and credit card become essential elements of the equipment at an independent contractor's disposal. Sometimes, transporting a weapon is too dangerous or maybe impossible due to state regulations. The independent contractor will therefore be obliged to make contact with a counterfeiter and with an illegal arms dealer before approaching the intended target . Forged documents and unregistered firearms are part of a dependence that unavoidably links the killer to a larger underworld network. This connection will be discussed in further detail in the chapter entitled "Postmodernity".

Failing to obtain forged documents would probably bring the unwanted attentions of investigators on the contractor: how comes that John Smith, a registered freelance translator, has traveled to and fro a number of US cities where murders very similar in the making – and apparently unconnected one with another – were committed?

Secrecy and disguise in our hi-tech society, however, require far more than forged documents. If the independent contractor wants to be successful, he or she must necessarily keep updated with the latest innovations in mobile technologies such as the internet and multimedia-enabled smartphones. These devices, albeit useful tools, may prove to be double-edged weapons as they can be easily tracked – apps like geo-tracking come immediately to mind – and constantly reveal the movements of the user. Computer literacy and the ability to interpret different roles, however, are not the sole skills required of an independent contractor; a number of less visible characteristics represent in fact his main "required traits". Not only the subject must be a cold, merciless killer, but he must also prepare the ground for the hit to occur.

> 'The really good hit man does his homework, making a complete study of his victim, his habits, his friends and associates, the

places he goes for a drink or to buy his morning paper. He will follow him for days and sometimes weeks, ascertaining what the victim's routine is, searching out potential locations for the hit, and, of course, ensuring that there is an escape route to get him away from the scene of the killing as swiftly and as calmly as possible.' (ibid.: 10)

Sometimes, the preparations are carried out so diligently that the independent contractor manages to disguise the murder as a suicide, or even as an accident. This outcome is often preferred by both the client and the killer, because it discourages authorities to put too much effort into the investigation (ibid.). Disguising a murder to make it pass like an accident is no small feat, neither, and it can only be done by a true professional. Moneywise, there certainly is a great difference between hiring a hoodlum and a professional killer to carry out a hit. As it has been demonstrated in the Horn case, in which the contractor hired an inexperienced thug to do the job of a pro, middle-class people have limited means when it comes to hire a killer. Although a liberated profession, killers – as any other highly specialized professional – have different fees depending on their curriculum vitae. Furthermore, hiring someone who is not up to the task can be very risky, as Kerr explains:

'[...] the amateur is a category of professional killer to be avoided at all costs. More often than not, he will already be involved in criminality, probably of a low-level kind.
'[...] he is likely to be already known to the police for his other activities. With DNA and the other forensic techniques available these days, one small error, one tiny detail will be enough to bring the law down on him and, eventually, you. And that is the second point – mistakes. The amateur, by his nature, is not going to carry out the action with the cold efficiency of the professional and he is usually caught.
'So, only hire the consummate professional. You will not have to

> do more than brief him, give him his money and wait. Within the time required to get it right, he will make his move, carry out his action and fade into the scenery as quickly as he emerged from it. He will be gone. Job done.' (ibid.: 12-13)

On this grounds, it becomes clear that although democratized, hired murder – fortunately – still fails to provide its middle-class customers with an insurance policy for not getting caught. Independent contractors – as it will be seen in the following section – have become available to the broader public, but the majority of potential clients still does not possess the financial means nor the necessary knowledge to hire a professional, and often contract the services of low-life criminals looking to hit the jackpot with one job.

an independent contractor. The 'sense of themselves' to which Pakulski and Waters refer to (1996), appears to be so varied and multifaceted, and follows such a 'disorderly personal order', that the sole person able to discern its full extent will, with all probability, be the individual to which the identity belongs to. If no one understands his identity, and if he does not feel represented by any social class in particular, then the individual will feel less constraints beyond the ones he consciously and unconsciously set for himself. The way in which the postmodern loss of a defined social class encouraged lower social classes, traditionally left out from the business of hired murder – a realm that used to belong to political and criminal affiliation systems alone – to join the game, becomes evident under these circumstances. Postmodernism, and the loosening of affiliations and shattering of fixed social identities it has caused, has contributed, along with increased wealth and access to modern information and transportation technologies, to the democratization of hired murder.

To quote anew the research conducted by Mouzos and Venditto (2003), its results have revealed that the majority of hits in Australia do not fall into criminal schemes, but may be considered as "crimes of passion" since they involve breakups, cheatings, and other aspects of relationships. How ironic that an offended lover would seek the aid of a cold-blooded killer to solve a sentimental heartache. Other cases analyzed by researchers at the Australian Institute of Criminology involved money, general revenge and criminal activities. According to this study, the average payment asked by Australian independent contractors ranges from an astonishingly low $387 to $76,000. In the United Kingdom, instead, by the late '90s prices ranged from 1,000 to 20,000 pounds per murder (The Independent, 1997). We may assume that these rates skyrocketed because of the past years' inflation. However, for high these sums may be – and regardless of the global financial crisis – they are still affordable by a rather large section of the population. Twenty thousand pounds equals the price of a car, and considering the affordability of a hit, the slogan utilized by professional killers – emulating former US President Hoover's words – could be: "A chicken in every pot, a murder in every garage." Hiring an independent contractor to carry out personal vendettas certainly represents the most glaring example of the thesis supported by this paper.

To sustain the argument made by the Australian Institute of Criminology, that is the majority of hits carried out by professional killers are related to crimes of passion, a number of cases will now be listed, beginning with an attempted assassination occurred in the city of sin itself, Las Vegas. In January 2011, Keith Harriman, 48 years old, hired an independent contractor in the attempt to murder his own son, guilty for having sex with both his stepmother and his father's ex-girlfriend. The proverbial "icing on the cake" came when the prodigal son – who has an extensive criminal record – after having a heated discussion with his father, reported him to the authorities over an insurance fraud scheme in which the man was involved in 2009. The report convinced Mr. Harriman that it was time to hire a professional killer and dispose of his beloved son, who miraculously survived after being shot 12 times in the body (Las Vegas Review Journal, 2011). This case is of particular relevance to this paper, because it shows how a) Mr. Harriman, answering only to his own whims and regardless of societal taboos, was willing to murder his own son; and that b) moved by a strong emotion like hate, Mr. Harriman somehow managed to keep a cold state of mind and have recourse to the services of an independent contractor, rather than carrying out the hit himself. This case is explanatory of how independent contractors seem to be meddled into the petty affairs of middle-class people far more often than grand political intrigues. But money and relationships are not the only causes that push people to seek the services of a hit man. Take Cory Trojano, 16, for example. When Mr. and Mrs. Trojano grounded him for getting bad grades at school and forbade him from playing to PlayStation 3, Cory resolved it was high time to terminate his parents. Warned by the exceedingly odd behavior shown by their son and aware of his threats, Mr. and Mrs. Trojano contacted the local police department, which provided the couple with an undercover cop who pretended to be an independent contractor all along. When Cory finally met the undercover cop to discuss the details of the hit in a hotel room, he was seized and taken into custody by the police (The Sunday Times, 2007). Leaving aside the sense of alienation given by adolescence and the postmodern fragmentation of identity that has been discussed at the beginning of this section, this case clearly shows how people, albeit in the darkest corner of their minds and highly dependent on the circumstances, think of assassination as an easy way out from a situation they perceive as unbearable. If personal "justice" has been made available to the general public, and provided that the aspiring client has access to it and the means to pay, without a defined identity to restrain him, what should keep him from making use of its service? Besides, it may be assumed that if Cory Trojano had not been so boastful on his intentions and planned the hit with due care, he might as well have been successful in having both his parents murdered by an independent contractor and maybe get away with it.

Young Cory Trojano's failure proves that those individuals who are willing to hire an independent contractor must have, at the very least, a general knowledge of their locality's underworld. Knowing where to go and who to ask for are fundamental first steps that will eventually lead the aspiring client to issue a death warrant for an unknowing victim. In spite of the stereotyped idea of a meeting taking place in the backdoor of a shadowy pub, Scotland Yard's officials maintain that some of the independent contractors they managed to get hold of admitted to have been initially approached in very unsuspicious places, such as public parks, cafés, etcetera (The Independent, 1997). Next time we go walking our dog, then, we might want to pay attention to what is being said by those people feeding ducks by the pond.

Once the initial approach has been made, the client and the independent contractor discuss the victim's habits and whereabouts, strategy, and - of course - reward. The victim, as it has been discussed in the previous sections, must be as detached as possible from the killer carrying out the hit. Sometimes, the client goes as far as the other hemisphere to follow this basic rule. In one of the most extraordinary known cases, two men hired a Maori hit woman from New Zealand for pounds 7,000 to murder a London roofing contractor with whom they had a business feud. Te Rangimaria Ngarimu, 27, was jailed for life in December 1994 for shooting her victim four times in the head and body (The Independent, 1997). This case highlights the degree of globalization reached by professional killers: through a vast web of underground networks, independent contractors and clients are able to meet each other's demands no matter the physical distance. A Maori hit woman in downtown London is as exotic as professional murder can get.

Before focusing on the modern outreach of independent contractors, it is fair to spend a few words on the increasing percentage of women undertaking this criminal profession. In spite of the media's intense coverage of female independent contractors, hit women have been around for longer than it is generally thought. Throughout history, there have been several cases where a hit woman was caught murdering or attempting to murder an important public figure or a businessman. Ninjas, for example, had no qualms in hiring women and training them to become efficient spies and killers; they were called Kunoichi, and they were as deadly or perhaps even deadliest than their male counterparts (Turnbull, 2007). In more recent times, the legendary figure of Mata Hari (real name Margaretha Geertruida "Grietje" Zelle), a Dutch exotic dancer allegedly employed by the French and German secret services respectively during World War I, came to represent the archetype of femme fatale (Howe, 1986). However, listing all or at least some of the known hit women who have left their mark in history would make a book on its own altogether. Moreover, as in the case of hit men, academic sources in regards to hit women are extremely scarce and often cloaked in legend. For example, in the years 2000 and 2001, famed newspapers such as The Observer, The Times, The Sunday Telegraph and The Daily Mail published a number of articles according to which then-dictator of Iraq Saddam Hussein was deploying a special unit of women specifically trained to carry out political assassinations. This group of women, came to be known by the infamous name of "female death squad", would have traveled as far as Denmark and Britain to approach and murder Iraqi and Kurdish dissidents of the régime. Among the strategies allegedly utilized by these hit women, were belly dancing and seduction, apparently the secret weapons at the disposal of a femme fatale. As in the case of their illustrious predecessor, the Dutch exotic dancer Mata Hari who was – with all probability – unjustly accused of treason and sentenced to death in a rather inelegant attempt by the French secret service to cover up a scandal involving another agent, most journalists today admit that the "female death squad" was yet another attempt by a number of newspapers and politicians to demonize Saddam Hussein during the months preceding the Second Gulf War (Monck, 2007).

That is to say, you may take politics out of professional murder, but you can't take professional murder out of politics. The nexus between hit men and politics is still regarded, by the public opinion and the Medias, as an inescapable one. In fact, when lacking a political (secret agents and spies), criminal (gangsters) or psychological motive (serial killers), professional killers enter a realm that academics have thus far largely ignored. Female independent contractors make no exception to this rule, and what is known about how they operate always comes in the form of a second-hand reference from manuals dedicated to serial killers or femme fatales. However, taking into consideration the particular case of Te Rangimaria Ngarimu, it might be assumed that female independent contractors operate pretty much in the same way as men do. In a way, their gender – still regarded by large sections of the populace as one exclusively fitting housework, caring and fostering – may even constitute an advantage when carrying out a contract. As an experienced actress, the hit woman could draw great advantage from the stereotypical image surrounding her gender, and approach the victim in a much easier and less-suspicious way as a male counterpart ever could. Therefore, it is safe to assert that the role of women in professional murder constitutes another example of how assassination has undergone a process of democratization, in favor of independent contractors and clients alike.

In regards to the degree of mobility and delocalization reached by modern independent contractors, instead, it must be asserted that Assassins and Ninjas were no strangers to traveling to faraway countries to fulfill a contract; however, never before in the history of assassination had killers journeyed as far as another hemisphere to kill. The globalization of professional murder has been driven by modern communication and transportation technologies, thanks to which communicating and traveling to and fro the other side of the planet may take as little as one day. The technological advancements have changed the way in which we perceive reality, to a point that

> 'a person's relationships and forms of interaction become increasingly unconstrained by geography and are no longer necessarily 'local' or 'national' in nature'. (Inglis, 2012: 268)

Furthermore, globalization would create relationships that do not require a physical presence of the actors (Giddens, 1991 cited in Inglis, 2012). An obvious example of this is the internet, thanks to which people are able to write, talk and see each other live from as far as the diametrically opposite sides of the world. This new, virtual way of interacting with others across time and space has caused what the author calls a disembedding of social relations, which would be driven by factors such as money and "expert systems", where money

> 'provide for the enactment of transactions between agents widely separated in time and space' (ibid.: 24)

while "expert systems" are

> 'systems of technical accomplishment or professional expertise that organise large areas of the material and social environments in which we live today'. (ibid.. 27)

Together, these two factors hold the capacity to 'remove social relations from the immediacies of context ... by providing "guarantees" of expectations across distanciated time-space' (ibid.: 28).

The money offered by the aspiring client and the "expert system" provided by an independent contractor constitute just one of such disembedded social relations, where the advantage of hiring a foreign independent contractor is furthered by the given "guarantee of expectations".

This point becomes even more prominent in the light of our current postmodern age, as a constant state of transition defines human movements and relationships across the globe. With very little preparation on his or her part, an independent contractor may therefore leave from and arrive at the most standardized artificial setting currently existing on Earth, that is the airport, a "switching-yard" for peoples coming, going, or simply passing by. Among thousands of tourists, businesspeople, workers, hostesses and stewards, the independent contractor easily passes as a regular traveler. Using English as a passepartout language to rent a car and reach his first destination, with all probability an unglamorous chain hotel he has booked long in advance from the comfort of his house, the independent contractor displays the pieces of the puzzle on his freshly made bed: a note reporting the address of the victim, another with some numbers to call in case he needs to obtain an unregistered firearm, a few photographs, and a map of the city. If the independent contractor is up to date with technology, which we assume he is considering how important a role it plays in his profession, then he probably stores all the information in his personal smartphone. Not only a mobile device permits the independent contractor to easily store and consult a large quantity of data, but it may also be protected with a password and – most importantly – deleted with a click. After setting up his temporary base in a hotel room, the independent contractor proceeds to the following step of his contract, which consists in the localization and study of his victim. The stalking of the victim is carried out with the most unsuspicious attitude made possible by the case, and this aspect presents two important elements characteristic of Assassins and Ninjas combined together: craftiness and stealth. In the days following the localization of the victim, the professional killer begins a careful observation of his habits and movements, and only when he is certain about his daily routine he prepares to strike. The hit often occurs with a firearm, always the first choice for professional killers (Mouzos and Venditto, 2003). However, the perfect murder is the one that is mistaken by officers for an accident. In this case, the art of sabotaging, of which Ninjas were true masters, becomes extremely valuable.

Passing the murder as an accident is, however, very difficult, and some independent contractors prefer to focus on disposing of the victim instead and making a safe escape, as far from police investigations as possible. Escape must occur in the quickest and least suspicious way possible and independent contractors – as it has been mentioned in "The required traits of a hit man" – put a lot of effort into this purpose. The "Plan B" is the trademark of a real pro, as it is assumable that a person who kills for a living has done so many other times before and will keep doing it long afterwards. To this day, however, amateurish professional killers do not place as much attention as escaping requires, and this lack of attention threatens to put the entire operation in jeopardy. Getting caught obviously means going to jail, but it also means betraying the trust of the client, as at this point the independent contractor may want to confess everything to the police in the hope of receiving a remission. Differently from Assassins and Ninjas, modern hit men have neither loyalty nor ideal to live up to, and the client may discover this simple yet potentially fatal fact on their own skin.

Leaving a country, however, is no longer as easy as hopping on a horse and ride as fast as you can; in our time, there are certain procedures that need to be followed, official documents to be shown, and security checks to pass in order to cross a national border. The independent contractor must prepare all these steps carefully in advance if he wishes to make his escape without incurring in any problem. As in the case of obtaining unlicensed firearms, his knowledge of the locality's underworld may prove providential, as for in exchange of a certain sum of money (or a favor), a "wiseguy" living in the territory of the hit could help him escape the country as safely and unmolested as any tourist. Flying, for example, is by no means the only way out of a country entirely surrounded by water like the United Kingdom. Albeit the European Union has attempted to issue "measures aimed at enhancing the security of ships and port facilities in the face of threats of intentional unlawful acts" (Regulation EC, No 725/2004), thus increasing passport controls and ports inspections, whoever has gone on a cruise or traveled at least once on a ferry knows that such controls do not present the same rigorousness toward passengers as the ones carried out by airports security personnel. Most passengers embarking on a cruise ship report that the sole control they were subjected to was a pat on the shoulders and a welcoming smile. It might be argued that cruise companies already detain the personal information of the passenger before he even boards the ship; however, tickets may also be bought with cash from any travel agency or at the local ticket office, and in regards to official forms of identification, the underworld connections of the hit man can prove useful in yet another instance, as they may provide him with counterfeited documents. Therefore, in spite of modern security checks, there are still a number of ways for leaving a country as quickly and as safely as possible without raising any suspicion. And for this reason, upon completing the contract, we can picture the hit man enjoying a cruise under the sun of the Caribbean…

More often than not, an effect produces a counter effect. It is so that in order to fight and prevent international crime, police corps around the world have encouraged cooperation and formed a law enforcement network that crosses national borders. This commitment has promoted a continuous exchange of information among police corps worldwide, and special agents are now able – with due authorization – to chase a suspected criminal overseas. Interpol, an abbreviation that stands for "International Criminal Police Organization", certainly constitutes the best example of the effort made by the global judicial system to keep up with a world that is becoming more and more globalized, and criminal organizations that have consequently extended their operations throughout several nations at once. As Interpol's status reads:

> 'INTERPOL is the world's largest international police organization, with 188 member countries. Created in 1923, it facilitates cross-border police co-operation, and supports and assists all organizations, authorities and services whose mission is to prevent or combat international crime.
>
> INTERPOL aims to facilitate international police co-operation even where diplomatic relations do not exist between particular countries. Action is taken within the limits of existing laws in different countries and in the spirit of the Universal Declaration of Human Rights. INTERPOL's constitution prohibits 'any intervention or activities of a political, military, religious or racial character.' (Interpol, 2010)

Globalization has therefore had several implications, among which transforming the way crime is committed, investigated and – eventually – punished (Varese, 2011). By being allowed access to national police corps databases and archives, and thanks to their well-established international presence, Interpol agents are able to localize and chase a crime-offender no matter the geographical and political barriers. The best way to understand Interpol's global reach is to report a summary of their crime fight and prevention methods:

> 'identify, establish and maintain contacts with experts in the field; monitor and analyze information related to specific areas of activity and criminal organizations; identify major criminal threats with potential global impact; pursue strategic partnerships with various organizations and institutions; assist in finding solutions to problems encountered by law enforcement agencies (LEAs); evaluate and exploit information received at the General Secretariat from National Central Bureaus, LEAs, open sources, international organizations and other institutions; monitor open-source information and reports; initiate, prepare and participate in programs to improve the international sharing of information; promote and carry out joint projects with other international organizations and institutions active in specific crime areas; research, develop and publish documents for investigators; provide support to member countries in ongoing international investigations on a case-by-case basis.' (Interpol, 2010)

It goes without saying that the aforementioned methods have been specifically designed to fight criminal organizations such as Cosa Nostra, Yakuza and the Drug Cartels. Nevertheless, the underworld network is a galaxy of organized crime associates, freelancers and smalltime criminals. When fulfilling a contract, independent contractors may be following their own personal gain, wholly detached from a gang's agenda; however, in order to obtain the necessary equipment (forged documents, unregistered firearms, etc.) and contacts to plan a safe escape out of the country of the hit, the freelance professional killer needs to make the acquaintance of people who, with all probability, have ties to organized crime. The highly romanticized image of the solitary professional killer who works with no one except his own firearm must be discarded in favor of a criminal with a widely extended web of connections: firstly, the independent contractor cannot open an "Hired Murder Inc." in the style of a real estate agency, and must delegate to others the responsibility of making the first approach with potential customers and eventually come to an agreement; second, as it has been mentioned before, he must obtain forged documents and unregistered firearms, domains traditionally belonging to criminal organizations; lastly, wise-guys on the territory of the hit will grant him a safe way out of the crime scene. These three elements make any independent contractor look more like "a nobody with good connections" rather than an all-knowing jack-of-all-trades (The Star, 2009).

As the activities of an independent contractor increase in intensity and his reach extends to every part of the globe, so does his need to maintain a vast list of underworld contacts become vital. This fact gives rise to a question that has preoccupied crime experts for decades: does an improvement in the efficiency of police corps consequentially result into criminals "battening down the hatches" to face the new challenge? The same could hold true for police corps facing the dire necessity to keep up with an ever-evolving crime. Unity, for good and for worse, is therefore a common need for both police agents and criminals, and independent contractors, in spite of a broad romantic literature existing on their account, make no exception to this rule.

VI
Conclusion

Starting from the historical origins of hired murder, this paper has discussed how the figure of the professional killer has evolved throughout the millennia from being the "left hand of God" and an undercover agent at the service of plotting nobles and underworld organizations, to become a full-fledged criminal exclusively devout to money.

The significance of postmodernity and globalization have also been examined, as society and the way it is perceived by individuals is currently being reshaped by the relentless advancement in transportation and communication technologies that, together with a steady rise in the global wealth per capita (Kharas, 2010) and democratization of the masses, is providing hundreds of millions of people around the world with opportunities, commodities and desires undreamt of until the early aftermath of World War II in industrialized nations, and more recently in industrializing countries, where the initial phases of rapid urbanization cause a general increase in crime (Gurr, 1981).

By making reference to a number of newspaper articles reporting on recent cases of assassinations or attempted assassinations carried out by professional killers, and researches undertook by prestigious institutions such as the Australian Institute of Criminology, this paper has tried to explain (1) how and why hired murder is becoming available to an increasingly wider and more heterogeneous public, and (2) what role globalization plays into such an historical transformation in the availability and understanding middle-class people have of murder through the formation of complex "disembedded" identities and the obtainment of increasingly higher financial means. Elements like the role of violence and a military background in the upbringing of an independent contractor, along with gender and other characteristics have also been discussed in the attempt to provide the paper with a solid and varied background of professional killers that would ultimately frame the topic of this paper within a context made of real people, real problems, and real murders.

Bibliography

- Adams, Andy (1966). 'A turbulent era spawns a deadly... breed', Black Belt Vol. 4, Number 12, pp. 14-21 . Active Interest Media Inc.

- Baldwin, Tom (2007). Mother's sting catches son, Cory Ryder, "hiring hitman to kill her." The Times [online] available at <http://www.timesonline.co.uk/tol/news/world/us_and_americas/article2789073.ece> [Accessed 20 August, 2011]

- Bandiera, Oriana (2001). Private States and the Enforcement of Property Rights: Theory and evidence on the origins of the Sicilian mafia, London School of Economics, CEPR Discussion Papers 3123

- European Committee Regulation No 725/2004 of the European Parliament and of the Council of 31 March 2004 on enhancing ship and port facility security

- Fein, R.A. and Vossekuil B. (1999). 'Assassinations in the United States: an Operational Study of Recent Assassins, Attackers, and Near-Lethal Approachers', Journal of Forensic Studies, Vol. 44(2), pp.321-333

- Feral, Rex (1983). Hit Man: A Technical Manual for Independent Contractors. Paladin Press

- Gens, Xavier (2007). Hitman. 20th Century Fox

- Giddens, Anthony (1991) Modernity and Self Identity: Self and Society in the Late Modern Age. Cambridge, Polity

- Gribben, Mark (n.d.). Murder Inc., Crime Library: Criminal Minds and Methods [online] available at: <http://www.trutv.com/library/crime/gangsters_outlaws/gang/inc/1.html> [Accessed 19 June, 2011]

- Gurr, T. (1981) 'Historical Trends in Violent Crime', Crime and Justice: An Annual Review of Research, 3: 295–353

- Headley, L. and Hoffman, W. (1992). Contract Killer: The Explosive Story of the Mafia's Most Notorious Hitman Donald "Tony the Greek" Frankos. Thunder's Mouth Press, New York

- Hermann, Peter (April 24, 2009). Dead Man Inc. The Baltimore Sun [online] available at:

  <http://weblogs.baltimoresun.com/news/crime/blog/2009/04/dead_man_inc.html> [Accessed June 18, 2011]

- HITMAN – Professional Killings (Contract Killers and Assassins) [online] Available at: <http://hitman.us/main.html> [Accessed 23 June, 2011]

- Howe, Russel Warren (1986). Mata Hari: The True Story. New York: Dodd, Mead and Company.

- Kharas, Homi (2010). 'The Emerging Middle Class in Developing Countries', OECD Development Center, Working Paper No. 285

- Inglis, David (2012). An Invitation to Social Theory. Cambridge, Polity

- Interpol – International Criminal Police Organization [online] Available at: <http://www.interpol.int/default.asp> [Accessed July 23, 2011]

- Lupo, Salvatore (2009). History of the Mafia, Columbia University Press

- Kerr, G. (2008). Professional Killers. Futura

- Lewis, Bernard (2002). The Assassins: a radical sect in Islam, Basic Books

- McCabe, Francis (2011). Son testifies against father in murder-for-hire plot. Las Vegas Review-Journal [online] available at: <http://www.lvrj.com/news/son-testifies-against-father-in-murder-for-hire-plot-115155774.html> [Accessed 20 August, 2011]

- Mol, Serge (2003). Classical weaponry of Japan: special weapons and tactics of the martial arts, Kodansha

- Monck, Adrian (December 1, 2007). Reporting Iraq before the war: journalists, spies and belly dancers. Adrian Monck [online] available at: <http://adrianmonck.com/2007/12/reporting-iraq-before-the-war-journalists-spies-and-belly-dancers/> [Accessed 22 July, 2011]

- Mouzos, Jenny and Venditto, John (2003). "Contract Killings in Australia", Australian Institute of Criminology, Research and Public Policy Series No. 53

- Newton, Michael (2008). Criminal Investigations: Serial Killers, Infobase Publishing

- North, Douglass C. and Thomas, Robert Paul (1977).

"The First Economic Revolution", The Economic History Review Volume 30, Issue 2, pp. 229-241

- Ouellet, Martin (2009). Quebec contract killer pleads guilty to 27 counts of murder. The Star [online] available at: <http://www.thestar.com/news/canada/article/611270> [Accessed 25 July, 2011]

- Petacco, Arrigo (2004). L'Uomo della Provvidenza, Mondadori

- Qian, Siam (109-91 B.C.). "Biographies of the Assassins", Records of the Grand Historian or Shiji

- Servadio, Gaia (1978). Mafiosi, Dell

- Scott, Pelley (August 15, 2000). Mind Of The Assassin. CBS 60 minutes [online] (Last updated April 22 2007) available at: <http://www.cbsnews.com/stories/2007/04/22/60minutes/main2714959.shtml> [Accessed May 20, 2011].

- Smith, Van and Ericson, Jr. Edward (23 April, 2009). BGF Offers $10,000 for Hits, Prosecutor Says . Baltimore City Paper [online] available at: <http://www2.citypaper.com/news/story.asp?id=17950> [Accessed June 18, 2011]

- Suetonius, Gaius Tranquillus (2007). The Twelve Caesars, Penguin Group USA Incorporated

- Turnbull, Stephen (2007). Warriors of Medieval Japan, Osprey Publishing

- Turnbull, Stephen (2003). Ninja AD 1460-1650, Osprey Publishing

- Varese, Federico (2011). Mafias on the Move: How Organized Crime Conquers New Territories. Princeton University Press

- Vick, Karl (4 May, 1996). Horn Convicted for Three Murders. The Washington Post [online] available at: <http://www.washingtonpost.com/wp-srv/local/longterm/library/montgom/hitmen/horn.htm>

Biography

Jason Ray Forbus was born in Rome on December 17, 1984. A US-Italian dual citizen, Jason's complex and varied background developed, since his early childhood, into a love for traveling and a strong interest for other cultures, which led him to live, work and study in Italy, Spain, Sweden, the UK and the United States.

He holds a diploma in Arts and Communication (Arts High School "A. G. Bragaglia" in Cassino, Italy), a bachelor of arts in Languages and Literatures for Multimedia Communication (University of Cassino, Italy) and a master of science in Globalization (University of Aberdeen, United Kingdom). His professional experiences range from translator to media specialist.

Literature and writing have both played an important role in Jason's life since his early youth. Already in 2002, at the age of 16, the author successfully debuted in the national youth literary contest "Campiello", in which his short story "Trovare il Cercare" (*Finding the Search*) classified amongst the first 25 in Italy and first in the Lazio Region.

Since then, Jason has authored several publications in Italian, English, and translated into several other languages. His books in English include: The Revolt of the Skeletons in the Closet (youth novel), The Memory of Odin (novel) and Contract Killing in the Information Age (Criminology Essay).

Our Mission

The future depends on reading and imagination...
Neil Gaiman

Ali Ribelli Edizioni is an indie publishing house that, through the publication of graphic novels, comic books and illustrated novels, is returning the pleasure of travel through reading.

Their works are always original and visionary, capable of transporting the reader into wonderful, sometimes scary, scenarios that are always different and unpredictable, filled with dreams and nightmares.

They publish a dichotomy between black and white that is reflected in the genres being edited: the first, a bit dark, the second lighter and suitable for audiences of all ages.

Each piece published by Ali Ribelli, from the novel to the graphic novel, has an important, exclusive and valuable graphic contribution.

The same attention is paid to the selection of fascinating stories and the printing of each book that are always well researched and full of quality.

We are your publisher, and for you we combine art and writing... giving life to wonderful worlds where you lose yourself and have fun.

The Revolt of the Skeletons in the Closet

In the seemingly peaceful and pleasant town of Wolverhampton, England, an entrepreneur had the brilliant and terrifying idea of creating a Park of Horrors.

The idea was the brainchild of Sir Desrius – better known as the "Warlock" – a cruel and unscrupulous man who did not hesitate to imprison monsters and fairy creatures from every corner of the globe to populate the park.

For years now, the monsters have been forced to suffer abuse, yet for some time rumors have spread of a rebellion…

Dedicated to those who are victims of prejudice, *The Revolt of the Skeletons in the Closet* is a fairy tale that speaks straight to the heart of young and old alike.

The Final Reaping

Stay alert. Surrender not to the Crows. Sing freely, and let your voice shake the foundations of the world. The acclaimed graphic novel written by Jason R. Forbus and illustrated by Boris and Daria Sokolovsky available in a masterfully compiled eBook.

Made in the USA
Columbia, SC
28 October 2021

47964998R00048